D1413579

VOICES OF WAR

World War I
The War to End All Wars

Enzo George

Cavendish Square
New York

Published in 2015 by Cavendish Square Publishing, LLC
243 5th Avenue, Suite 136, New York, NY 10016

© 2015 Brown Bear Books Ltd

First Edition

Website: cavendishsq.com

This publication represents the opinions and views of the author based on his or her personal experience, knowledge, and research. The information in this book serves as a general guide only. The author and publisher have used their best efforts in preparing this book and disclaim liability rising directly or indirectly from the use and application of this book.

CPSIA Compliance Information: Batch #WS14CSQ

All websites were available and accurate when this book was sent to press.

Library of Congress Cataloging-in-Publication Data
George, Enzo.
World War I : the war to end all wars / Enzo George.
     pages cm. — (Voices of war)
Includes index.
ISBN 978-1-62712-861-2 (hardcover) ISBN 978-1-62712-863-6 (ebook)
1. World War, 1914-1918—History—Juvenile literature. I. Title.

D522.7.B45 2015
940.4—dc23

                          2014002028

For Brown Bear Books Ltd:
Editorial Director: Lindsey Lowe
Managing Editor: Tim Cooke
Children's Publisher: Anne O'Daly
Design Manager: Keith Davis
Designer: Lynne Lennon
Picture Manager: Sophie Mortimer
Production Director: Alastair Gourlay

Picture Credits:
Front Cover: Robert Hunt Library

All images **Robert Hunt Library** except:
Library of Congress: 8; **TopFoto**: 38.

Artistic Effects: Shutterstock

Brown Bear Books has made every attempt to contact the copyright holder. If you have any information please contact smortimer@brownbearbooks.co.uk.

We believe the extracts included in this book to be material in the public domain. Anyone having any further information should contact licensing@windmillbooks.co.uk.

Manufactured in the United States of America

CONTENTS

German troops on the Western Front relax in their underground bunker in 1916.

Introduction

Around 1900, European nations formed two groups. On the one hand were the Allies, comprised of Britain, France, and Russia. On the other were the Central Powers, who were Germany and Austria-Hungary. In June 1914, the assassination of an Austrian archduke in Serbia triggered the mobilization of troops in Serbia's ally, Russia. Austria-Hungary's ally, Germany, also mobilized. German plans for war depended on defeating France before fighting Russia. When German troops invaded Belgium in August 1914, heading for France, France and Britain declared war. Soon, the Turkish Ottoman Empire joined the Central Powers and Italy joined the Allies. Europe's colonies around the world also joined the conflict.

In the West, the Allies stopped the German advance on Paris. Both sides dug long lines of trenches, from which they faced each other. In the East, Germany managed to defeat Russia by 1917.

Hundreds of U.S. lives were lost on ships sunk by German submarines in the Atlantic Ocean. Germany also tried to make an alliance with Mexico. In 1917, the United States declared war on the side of the Allies. The arrival of more than one million U.S. troops in France helped overcome the stalemate on the Western Front. With its armies being pushed back and the country on the edge of revolution, Germany surrendered on November 11, 1918. The war was finally over.

U.S. troops and supplies arrive in France after the United States joined the war in April 1917.

WAKE UP, AMERICA!

CIVILIZATION CALLS
EVERY MAN WOMAN AND CHILD!

MAYOR'S COMMITTEE 50 EAST 42" ST

The U.S. government set out to involve all parts of society in the war effort.

War Breaks Out in Europe

After the murder of Archduke Franz Ferdinand, Austria-Hungary declared war on Serbia. Russia, a Serb ally, mobilized its armies. That led Germany to activate the Schlieffen Plan. The plan was designed to avoid having to fight on two fronts at the same time. It called for Germany to defeat France before facing Russia.

Excited German troops leave for the front in a railroad truck labeled "Outing to Paris."

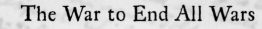

Austrians celebrate the declaration of war in Vienna. They are holding up portraits of the Austrian and German rulers.

❝ Unbelievably large crowds are waiting outside the newspaper offices. News arrives in the evening that Serbia is rejecting the ultimatum. General excitement and enthusiasm, and all eyes turn toward Russia—is she going to support Serbia?

The days pass from July 25 to 31. Incredibly exciting; the whole world is agog to see whether Germany is now going to mobilize. I've hardly got enough peace of mind left to go to the bank and do my trainee job. I play truant as though it were school and stand about all day outside the newspaper offices, feeling that war is inevitable. **❞**

Herbert Sulzbach, a German Army reservist, recorded in his diary the mood in Frankfurt on July 24, 1914.

OUTBREAK OF WAR FACTS

- Austria-Hungary issued an ultimatum to Serbia after the assassination. When it was rejected, Austria-Hungary declared war on July 28, 1914.
- Russia ordered a partial mobilization on July 29 to support Serbia; Germany mobilized on July 30.
- On August 2, German troops invaded Belgium on their way into France.
- France declared war on Germany on August 3, when Germany also declared war on Russia.
- On August 4, Britain declared war. This also brought the countries of its empire, from Australia to Canada, into the war.

The Armies Mobilize

The opposing forces had to raise large armies. There were many volunteers for what people thought would be a short war. As the conflict went on, countries also introduced conscription, or forced military service. In Britain, the Secretary of War, Lord Kitchener, encouraged volunteers by organizing "Pals' battalions," in which friends served together.

A U.S. recruiting poster urges men to join up before they are drafted.

" We are a mixed lot—a triumph of democracy. Some of us have fifty years to our credit and only own to thirty; others are sixteen and claim to be eighteen. Some of us enlisted for glory, and some for fun, and a few for fear of starvation. Some of us began by being stout, and have lost weight; others were seedy and are filling out. Some of us grumble, and go sick to escape parades; but for the most part we are aggressively cheerful, and were never fitter in our lives.

Battle! Battle, murder, and sudden death! Maiming, slaughter, blood, extremities of fear and discomfort and pain! How incredibly remote all that seems! We don't believe in it really. It is just a great game we are learning. It is part of the game to make little short rushes in extended order, to lie on our bellies and keep our heads down, snap our rifles and fix our bayonets. Just a game, that's all, and then home to tea. "

Donald Hankey was still a student when he enrolled in the British Army early in the war. The horrors of trench warfare were still to become apparent.

RECRUITMENT FACTS

- At the start of the war, Russia mobilized nearly 6 million men and France just over 4 million. Germany mobilized 4.5 million men, and Austria-Hungary a further 3 million. The British Army numbered fewer than 1 million.
- At the start of the war, Britain was the only major European nation that did not have conscription.
- Britain introduced conscription in 1916.
- The United States introduced conscription with the Selective Service Act in May 1917.

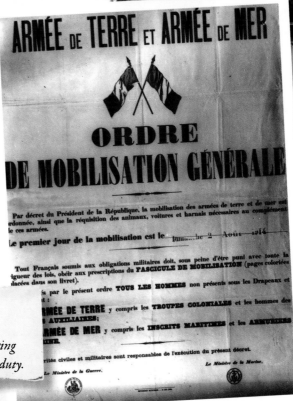

Posters were put up throughout France on August 1, 1914, ordering reservists to report for duty.

Life in the Trenches

After the German advance on Paris was defeated, the Western Front settled into stalemate. The two sides faced each other from heavily defended trenches. For nearly four years, the trench lines stayed largely in the same place. Both sides launched occasional huge attacks across "no-man's land," but the front barely moved.

British engineers in a flooded trench. Constant damp caused a condition known as trench foot.

TRENCH FACTS

- The enemy front line trenches were usually 100 to 300 yards apart (90–275 m), but were sometimes closer.
- Front line trenches were connected by communications trenches to the support trenches where soldiers slept and ate.
- Trenches were about 12 feet (3.5 m) deep. A fire step meant soldiers could look over the parapet.
- Trench walls might be supported by wood or sandbags. The floor was usually covered by wooden boards.
- The trenches stretched over 400 miles (640 km). Each side built over 12,000 miles (19,300 km) of trenches in the war.

" There are those who deny that breakfast is the most important meal of the day, but in the trenches no-one could question it for a moment. No matter how violent, sulfurous, or bloody the night, no matter how grim the ceremonial of 'stand to' which ushered in the day, the command 'stand down' was almost invariably followed by a lull along the whole front. Hostilities were temporarily suspended by mutual, if mute, consent.

For anything from an hour to two hours the most vicious noise to be heard in the trenches was the sizzling of frying bacon. Then some machine-gunner, cheerful from his meal, would break the spell with the 'Pop-pop-op-pop-pop!' call on his Vickers, which never failed to evoke the slower 'pop-pop' from some heavy machine-gun within the German lines. "

British infantryman Sidney Rogerson describes how life in the trenches soon took on its own daily routines, even with time for breakfast.

Going Over the Top

With the war bogged down in the trenches, generals had little idea how to make a breakthrough. Commanders tried a series of head-on attacks by the infantry. Following an artillery barrage on enemy lines, whistles blew and the men went "over the top" into no-man's land—and often into a hail of machine-gun fire. Few such attacks succeeded for long. Millions of men died for little territorial gain.

British infantry leave a temporary trench during an advance at the Battle of Arras in April 1917.

German troops leave their trench during an attack in the Battle of Lys in September 1917.

" At 4.15 a whistle blew. The men in the front line went over the top, and we scrambled out and took their places in the front trench. In front of us was a small field… split diagonally by an old footpath. On the other side of the field was a belt of trees in which lay the Hun [German] trench. In a few moments flags went up there, to show that it had been captured and that the troops were going on.

Another whistle, and we ourselves scrambled over the parapet and sprinted across the field. Personally I was so overweighted that I could only amble [walk slowly]. I took the diagonal path, as the line of least resistance, and most of my section did the same.

When I dropped into the Hun trench I found it a great place, only 3 feet (90 cm) wide, and at least 8 (2.4 m) deep, and beautifully made of white sandbags, back and front. At that spot there was no sign of any damage by our shells, but a number of dead Huns lay in the bottom. There was a sniper's post just where I fell in, a comfortable little square hole, fitted with seats and shelves, bottles of beer, tinned meats, and a fine helmet hanging on a hook. "

Henry S. Chapman, a British infantryman, recalls going "over the top" in an attack at Givenchy, France, on June 19, 1915.

NO-MAN'S LAND FACTS

- The space between the front lines was known as no-man's land; it was covered in mines, barbed wire, and shell craters.
- No-man's land was often muddy. There was no vegetation, because all grass and trees had been destroyed by shelling.
- Patrols left the enemy trenches under cover of darkness to try to plant mines or lay or repair barriers of barbed wire.
- Infantry attacks were often preceded by a creeping barrage. This was a curtain of artillery fire that moved steadily ahead of the infantry to distract the enemy.
- Advancing troops communicated with their lines by telephone joined by wires.

Trying to Get Home

Tired British soldiers rest in shelters dug into the side of their trench.

Life in the trenches had long periods of boredom interrupted by bursts of sheer terror and the constant threat of death from an artillery shell. In such circumstances, many soldiers suffered a nervous breakdown. Some suffered a traumatized state known as shell shock. Others tried to get themselves wounded just badly enough to be sent home to recover.

British troops take cover in a trench during an artillery attack on the Western Front.

" I was moving down this support line having a word with one or two of our fellows and then I came to bays where there was nobody at all.

So I went very carefully round the next bend and I saw one of our battalion lads laid out on the ground on top of the parapet with his legs up in the air. And I said, 'What are you trying on?'

He said, 'Well I'm trying to get a wound if I can in my legs. There's quite a bit of machine-gunning going on and a few rifle fires. I thought I might get a bullet through my leg and get home to Blighty' [England].

I said, 'Get down, old lad, and forget about it, and I'll forget about it and your name will never pass my lips. We all feel exactly like you.'

He said, 'No, you don't feel like me.'

I says, 'Oh yes, we do, every one of us, but as we have a job to do, we're going to do it.' So I said, 'You go back to your mates,' which he did. And we were very big friends after that because we had a secret that nobody else knew. "

British soldier Eric Hare was worried that part of the trench his battalion was in might have been taken over by Germans.

TRENCH WARFARE FACTS

- Casualty rates in the trenches were high. Between 10 and 12 percent of all men who served on the front line were killed.
- Shell shock was first recognized in the trenches in 1914.
- Men in the trenches suffered a nervous and emotional breakdown and often became dazed or unable to walk or talk.
- A "blighty" wound was British slang for a wound that was not life-changing but was bad enough for a man to be sent back to Britain to recover.
- Many men lost limbs from mines or shelling; soldiers also often suffered burns in artillery explosions.

Gas Attack

In April 1915, the Germans introduced a new weapon at Ypres on the Western Front. They released chlorine gas that drifted on the wind toward the French lines. Although the Allies condemned the use of gas as a war crime, they also developed poison gas, which they first used in September 1915. Both sides soon developed protection against gas. This varied from damp cotton pads to place over the mouth to gas masks and respirators. Even horses wore gas masks.

This Australian chaplain wears a mask connected to a respirator that filters out harmful chemicals.

" From the base of the German trenches, over a considerable length, there appeared jets of whitish vapor, which gathered and swirled until they settled into a definite low cloud-bank, greenish-brown below and yellow above. This ominous bank of vapor drifted swiftly across the space which separated the two lines.

The French troops, staring over the top of their parapet at this curious screen which ensured them a temporary relief from fire, were observed suddenly to throw up their hands, to clutch at their throats, and to fall to the ground in the agonies of asphyxiation [choking]. **"**

The famous British writer Arthur Conan Doyle, the creator of Sherlock Holmes, witnessed the first gas attack at Ypres, Belgium, in April 1915.

GAS ATTACK FACTS

- The first poison gases were based on one of two main chemicals, chlorine or phosgene.
- Phosgene was introduced by the French in 1915. It had no color or smell, so it was harder to detect than chlorine and was a more effective weapon.
- In 1917 the Germans introduced mustard gas, which disabled soldiers by causing sickness and burns. It later caused internal bleeding and damaged the bronchial tubes, causing a slow death.
- Gas was never a particularly effective or decisive weapon, partly because it depended on the direction of the wind.

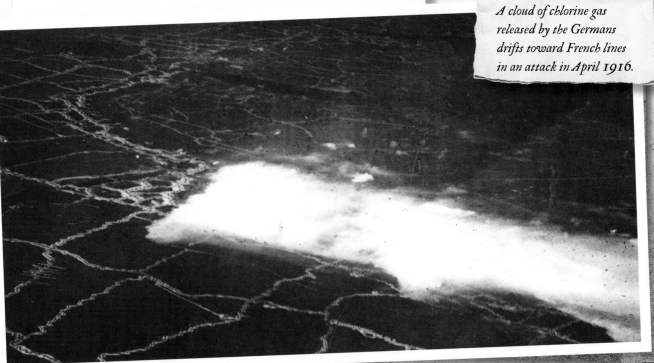

A cloud of chlorine gas released by the Germans drifts toward French lines in an attack in April 1916.

The Sinking of the *Lusitania*

In the Atlantic Ocean, German submarines targeted Allied ships carrying supplies to Britain. In February 1915, Germany announced that any ship in British waters was likely to be attacked. On May 7, 1915, a German submarine sank the passenger liner *Lusitania* near Ireland. Some 1,198 people died. The sinking caused outrage that Germany had broken an accepted rule of war not to attack civilians.

This German poster celebrates U-boat actions, even though submarine warfare was widely condemned as cowardly and unfair by the Allies.

A plume of water rises as a German torpedo strikes the side of an Italian steamer in the Atlantic Ocean.

" Just before the ship was struck, we were sitting at lunch, and as a girl friend was waiting for me I left the table before the others, and I never saw them again. I was in my cabin when the torpedo struck, and it seemed to hit a part of the boat near me. Instinctively I seemed to know we had been torpedoed, for it had been in all our minds right across the whole way, though it was treated mostly as a joke. We thought we got safely so far, all possible danger was past, but we made a terrible mistake. The smoke was already coming into my cabin, and I rushed above.

A great many people were running about, but others took it very quietly, though they were lowering the boats. It was everybody for themselves and I rushed down to the saloon to get a lifebelt but the steward would not give me one saying I was to go downstairs for one. "

Chrissie Aitken was 16 when she sailed from New York on *Lusitania* with her father, brother, and nephew. When the ship was torpedoed near Ireland, she was the only one of the party to survive.

NAVAL WAR FACTS

- German submarines were called U-boats, short for "Unterseeboot," the German word for the vessels.
- The sinking of the *Lusitania* caused outrage because a submarine had fired on an unarmed passenger vessel.
- It later emerged that *Lusitania* was carrying ammunition for the Allies.
- In January 1917 Germany introduced unrestricted submarine warfare.
- The sinking of three U.S. vessels on March 17 finally brought the United States into the war the following month.

Gallipoli

Allied troops are evacuated from Suvla Bay, Gallipoli, in December 1915. More than 35,000 men were evacuated.

In an effort to break the deadlock on the Western Front, the Allies planned an attack on Germany's ally, Ottoman Turkey. After a naval campaign in the Dardanelles strait, Allied divisions landed on the Gallipoli peninsula on April 25, 1915. Many came from the Australian and New Zealand Army Corps (ANZAC). The landings became bogged down on narrow beaches. After eight months and the loss of thousands of lives, the Allies were evacuated on December 15, 1915.

> 66 There was not much sudden death, but there was slow death everywhere. The body was slowly dying from the inside. We talked to each other; we laughed occasionally, but always the thought of death was in our minds—our insides were dying slowly. The water was death; the bully beef was death; everything was death. I was afraid to eat a thing. A man would pass me holding his stomach, groaning in agony, and a few minutes later I would take him off the latrine, dead. The men contracted dysentery and fever every day. The bullets did not take a big toll. It was the death of germs.
>
> The company had been in the line 25 days; it was a record. There was no talk about going out for a rest; there was nowhere to go, only down to the beach, and the beach was shelled incessantly. It was safer in the line. 99

Sergeant W. H. Leach served in the Canadian 1st Newfoundland Regiment at Gallipoli.

GALLIPOLI FACTS

- The Gallipoli Peninsula was selected because it would allow Allied troops to attack the Turkish capital, Constantinople (now Istanbul).
- The Allies landed on six beaches on April 25, 1915
- Only a prompt reaction by a Turkish officer named Mustafa Kemal stopped the different landing forces moving inland and joining up.
- In all, 570,000 British, Empire, and French troops served at Gallipoli.
- The role of the ANZACs is still marked in Australia and New Zealand, where Anzac Day is an important annual holiday.

Australian soldiers attack Turkish positions over rough, hilly ground typical of the Gallipoli peninsula.

The Christmas Truces

Two German soldiers pose with their British enemies during the Christmas truce in 1914.

The routine of life in the trenches was broken at Christmas. In 1914 a widespread unofficial truce broke out on Christmas Day, and soldiers from both sides mingled in no-man's land. However, such fraternization was strongly condemned by the military authorities. Although there were other truces a year later, they were not so widespread. By Christmas 1916, a year of bitter fighting and orders against mixing with the enemy ensured that there were no further truces.

German and English troops meet in no-man's land on Christmas Day, 1914.

❝ As soon as it became light, we saw hands and bottles being waved at us. A drunken German stumbled over his parapet and advanced through the barbed wire, followed by several others, and in a few moments there was a rush of men from both sides, carrying tins of meat, biscuits, and other commodities for barter. This was the first time I had seen no-man's land and now it was Every Man's Land, or nearly so. Some of our men would not go; they gave terse and bitter reasons for their refusal. The officers called our men back to the line, and in a few minutes no-man's land was once again empty and desolate. There had been a feverish exchange of 'souvenirs,' a suggestion for peace all day and a football match in the afternoon, and a promise of no rifle-fire at night. All this came to naught. **❞**

Lleweylln Wyn Griffith of the Royal Welsh Fusiliers was in a trench at Mametz Wood on Christmas Day, 1915.

TRUCE FACTS

- There had been public campaigns for an official Christmas truce, but the military authorities rejected the idea.
- In 1914 an estimated 100,000 British and German troops joined unofficial ceasefires along the Western Front.
- Soldiers exchanged small gifts, such as cigarettes, and souvenirs, such as military insignia.
- Senior officers issued orders forbidding friendly relations with enemy soldiers.
- Brief unofficial truces were relatively frequent, as each side allowed the other to collect and bury its dead from no-man's land.

The U-Boat Campaign

The German U-boat campaign was aimed at stopping Britain receiving supplies from the United States. In 1916, and especially after the introduction of unrestricted submarine warfare in January 1917, U-boats sank many ships. The Allies began to group ships into convoys defended by warships, which dramatically cut the success of the U-boats.

The crew of U-49 watch the Italian ship Giovanni Albanesi *burn after an attack in April 1918.*

An Allied convoy crosses the Atlantic. Grouping ships together made them easier to defend with warships.

" All her decks were visible to me. From all the hatchways a storming, despairing mass of men were fighting their way on deck, grimy stokers, officers, soldiers, groom, cooks. They all rushed, ran, screamed for boats, tore and thrust one another from the ladders leading down to them, fought for the lifebelts and jostled one another on the sloping deck. All among them, rearing, slipping horses are wedged. The starboard boats could not be lowered on account of the list; everyone therefore ran across to the port boats, which in the hurry and panic, had been lowered with great stupidity either half full or overcrowded. The men left behind were wringing their hands in despair and running to and fro along the decks; finally they threw themselves into the water so as to swim to the boats. "

Adolf von Spiegel was captain of *U-202*. In April 1916, he sank an Allied steamer carrying horses for the Western Front.

U-BOAT FACTS

- The Germans had 10 U-boats at the start of the war, but had brought another 395 into service by the end of the war.
- U-boats were too slow to be effective against most Allied warships.
- U-boats attacked more than 7,400 Allied vessels and sank nearly 5,000 ships, with a combined tonnage of 13 million tons.
- Allied measures to reduce the effectiveness of the U-boats included grouping ships into defended convoys, using depth charges, and laying barrages of underwater mines.
- 178 U-boats were sunk, with the loss of about 5,000 submariners.

First Day of the Somme

On July 1, 1916, the British began an offensive on the Somme River in France. The attack was one of the largest of the war, and one of the most bloody. Especially in Britain, the offensive became a symbol of the senseless sacrifice of the trenches. It confirmed many people's view that Allied generals were too ready to waste young lives.

British soldiers go over the top at Beaumont Hamel in a scene from a British movie of the battle made at the time.

A medic gives a drink to an injured British soldier during the attack.

" About 4 o'clock the order came to get ready for the attack. None could help thinking of what the next few hours would bring. One minute's anguish and then, once in the ranks, faces became calm and serene, a kind of gravity falling upon them, while on each could be read the determination and expectation of victory. Two battalions were to attack Belloy-en-Santerre, our company being the reserve. The companies forming the first wave were deployed on the plain. Bayonets glittered in the air above the corn, already quite tall. Alan's section formed the right and vanguard of the company and mine formed the left wing. After the first bound forward, we lay flat on the ground, and I saw the first section advancing beyond us and making toward the extreme right of the village.

I caught sight of Seeger and called to him. He answered with a smile. How pale he was! His tall silhouette stood out on the green of the cornfield. He was the tallest man in his section. His head erect, and pride in his eye, I saw him running forward, with bayonet fixed. Soon he disappeared and that was the last time I saw my friend. "

Rif Baer joined the Somme attack with his friend, the U.S. war poet Alan Seeger, who died in the attack.

SOMME FACTS

- The British Army lost nearly 20,000 troops on July 1, 1916, the single worst day in its history.
- A series of offensives on the Somme continued until October, with little gain for either side.
- Many French divisions intended for the Somme were diverted to resist the German siege at Verdun. At the Somme, the French played a supporting role for the British attack.
- Alan Seeger joined the French Foreign Legion so he could fight in the war.
- His most famous poem is entitled "I Have a Rendezvous with Death."

Medical Care

Trench warfare produced many casualties. Many soldiers were burned or lost limbs. Poison gas burned the skin, irritated the eyes, and damaged men's lungs. Shell shock was a form of emotional breakdown caused by intense stress. Sickness was common in the trenches. A particular problem was trench foot, a condition caused by standing for long periods in wet boots.

A wounded British soldier waits to be evacuated from an Advanced Dressing Station in November 1917.

Stretcher bearers move a casualty. Many stretcher bearers were volunteers.

> " For forty-eight hours we have been working without a stop, and still the fighting is going on, and the wounded are falling faster than we can pick them up. It has rained all week. The trenches are knee-deep—in some places waist-deep—with mud and water. The dead and wounded lie everywhere: in trenches, and shell pits, and along the sodden roads. Two thousand wounded have passed through our hands since the attack. Hundreds more are dying of exposure a mile away, and we cannot reach them. The wounded who are already here must lie outside the Dressing Station, in the open, under the rain, until their turn comes.
>
> We shall be relieved tonight, for twelve blessed hours, by the 3rd Field Ambulance. We are all in. "

Private Frank Walker served in the Canadian Medical Corps at Ypres. This extract from his diary is dated June 14, 1916.

MEDICAL CARE FACTS

- Initial medical care was provided at a Regimental Aid Post near the front line; from there, casualties were sent to an Advanced Dressing Station.
- More serious casualties were transferred by ambulance to a Casualty Clearing Station. These basic hospitals were the closest to the front line that female nurses were allowed to work.
- Further care was provided at general hospitals far behind the lines.
- The war brought great medical advances in prosthetics, the treatment of burns, and the diagnosis and treatment of traumatic stress disorders.

A New Weapon

British infantry examine a Mark II tank on the outskirts of Arras, France, in 1917.

British engineers developed tanks as a way to break through enemy trenches. The name "tank" was used as a code name to keep the vehicle's development secret from any German spies. The tank first appeared at the Somme in September 1916. Although tanks often broke down or became stuck, the British and French produced thousands of them and used them effectively.

66 We heard strange throbbing noises, and lumbering slowly towards us came three huge mechanical monsters such as we had never seen before. My first impression was that they looked ready to topple on their noses, but their tails and the two little wheels at the back held them down and kept them level. Big metal things they were, with two sets of caterpillar wheels that went right round the body.

There was a huge bulge on each side with a door in the bulging part, and machine guns on swivels poked out from either side. The engine, a petrol engine of massive proportions, occupied practically all the inside space. Mounted behind each door was a motorcycle type of saddle seat, and there was just about enough room left for the belts of ammunition and the drivers. 99

Bert Chaney, a private in the 7th London Territorial Battalion, remembers the first appearance of a tank in battle, September 15, 1916.

TANK FACTS

- The British Mark I tank was shaped like a rhombus, which helped it to cross obstacles such as wide trenches.
- Early tanks were highly unreliable and often broke down.
- The French built more tanks than all the other armies combined.
- The small French Renault FT was the first "modern" tank, with a heavy gun mounted in a rotating turret on the top.
- At the Battle of Cambrai in November 1917, British tanks broke through the German lines. The infantry failed to advance into the gap, however.

A British Mark IV tank looms over a German trench at Cambrai in November 1917.

On the Brink of War

President Woodrow Wilson was determined that the United States should be neutral in the war. But the sinking of the *Lusitania* in 1915 and of more U.S. vessels by German submarines in early 1917 changed U.S. public opinion. So did the revelation that the Germans would give Mexico U.S. territory if they sided with the Central Powers.

President Wilson addresses a joint session of Congress on April 2, 1917, asking for a delcaration of war.

As war loomed closer, the U.S. military began to try to persuade volunteers to increase its numbers.

❝ I had never seen him so worn down. He looked as if he hadn't slept, and he said he hadn't. He said he was probably going before Congress the next day to ask for a declaration of war, and he'd never been as uncertain about anything in his life as about that decision. For nights, he said, he'd been lying awake going over the whole situation—over the provocation given by Germany, over the probable feeling in the United States, over the consequences to the settlement and to the world at large if we entered the melee.

He said he couldn't see any alternative, that he had tried every way he knew to avoid war. 'I think I know what war means,' he said, and he added that if there were any possibility of avoiding war he wanted to try it. 'What else can I do?' he asked. 'Is there anything else I can do?'

I told him that his hand had been forced by Germany, that so far as I could see we couldn't keep out. **❞**

Newspaper editor Frank Cobb visited his friend Woodrow Wilson at the White House at 1:00 A.M. on April 2, 1917.

U.S. AT WAR FACTS

- In March 1917, five U.S. ships were sunk by German U-boats.
- A telegram from the German foreign minister offered Mexico territory in New Mexico, Texas, and Arizona in return for an alliance with Germany.
- On April 2, 1917, Wilson asked Congress to authorize a war "to make the world safe for democracy."
- Congress declared war on April 6, with the overwhelming backing of the public.

The Doughboys in Action

The commander of the American Expeditionary Forces, General John Pershing, insisted that his men—nicknamed the "Doughboys"—should be well trained before going to Europe. Only 14,000 U.S. troops had arrived in France by June 1917. They first saw action at Nancy in October. By May 1918, there were more than one million U.S. troops in France.

Men of the newly formed U.S. First Army bring munitions through the mud to the front at St. Mihiel in September 1918.

A U.S. machine-gun crew opens fire near St. Mihiel in September 1918.

" I saw one fellow drive a bayonet through a German, but before he could get it out, another German ran him through. A short jab and a quick withdrawal is the best.

The next German had one of our men in a fix. Our man had fallen and was grasping the German's bayonet with both hands trying to keep it from going into him. The bayonet was piercing the gas-mask bag on his chest. I yelled and rushed for the German. He saw me coming and swept his bayonet free from the fellow's grasp and swung stright for my head. I ducked low, but I must have thrown my rifle up because he struck my bayonet, knocking it to one side. From my crouching position I socked the rifle butt into his groin. It lifted him off his feet and he sank to the ground in a heap. It took all the wind out of me. "

William Scanlon was a Marine in the U.S. 2nd Division that attacked at St. Mihiel in September 1918.

DOUGHBOY FACTS

- U.S. infantry were nicknamed "doughboys" in the U.S.–Mexico War of 1846–1848.
- U.S. forces used French and British equipment, such as the Renault FT tank.
- The first U.S. actions were at Cantigny and Belleau Wood in May and June 1918.
- In June 1918 U.S. forces stopped a major German offensive at Château-Thierry and Belleau Wood.
- In September 500,000 U.S. soldiers attacked German positions at St. Mihiel.
- U.S. and French troops began an offensive in September 1918 that led to the German surrender.

The Air War

A German machine-gunner takes aim at a British two-winged biplane in this painting of a World War I dog fight.

Airplanes were used from the start of the war, mainly for observation purposes. Later, larger planes and airships named Zeppelins were used for bombing targets on the ground. A generation of fighter planes also evolved, armed with machine guns. Pilots known as "aces" fought dog fights high in the skies above the trenches. The dashing aces became popular heroes.

AIR WAR FACTS

- A pilot became an ace when he had achieved five proven "kills" against enemy aircraft.
- Eddie Rickenbacker led the U.S. aces, with 26 victories in 300 hours of flying.
- The highest number of kills was 80, by the German ace Baron Manfred von Richthofen, known as "the Red Baron."
- Rickenbacker and many of his U.S. colleagues flew the French-built Spad XIII fighter.
- The best-performing fighter of the war was the German Fokker D.VII, which was highly maneuverable and could climb and dive at steep angles.

" Not 50 yards in front of me I saw a whole flock of enemy Fokkers passing through a thin stratum of clouds. They had been lying in wait for out Spads without noticing me until I almost bumped into them. The next instant I was over on my wing and nose performing a double-quick spin out of their range.

All eight of them were on top of me firing as they followed my gyrations. Tracer bullets went whizzing past me every second and, try as I might, I could not select an opening that would permit me to slip through them with any hope of safety. The earth was rapidly coming up to meet me and the Fokkers were as ravenously bent on my destruction as ever when I opened up my motor and dove vertically toward the ground with throttle wide open. As I did so I was conscious that other machines were coming in from behind me and that the Fokkers had suddenly left off firing their beastly flaming bullets. Glancing back, I saw my own Spads had arrived in the very nick of time. "

Eddie Rickenbacker was the outstanding U.S. air ace of the war. He began flying his Spad airplane on the Western Front early in 1918.

Eddie Rickenbacker poses in the cockpit of his Spad XIII.

Discipline and Punishment

Military discipline in all armies was harsh. Cases of cowardice and desertion were taken before military courts for trial. Military courts were not only interested in the fate of the individual. They need to ensure that all troops understood that disobedience would be severely punished. Some deserters were condemned to be executed by firing squad.

A British firing squad prepares to execute a soldier for desertion.

A Russian officer threatens two deserters in an attempt to force them back to their posts.

" Just before dawn the sergeant shook the dozing soldiers. Stiff and silent they made their way to the quarry filling their lungs with the damp air. Many men are reported to have faced a firing squad bravely. This man, who had gone 'over the top' on 1st July, was not one of them. The waiting Manchesters saw the shirt-sleeved figure sway at the top of the quarry steps and watched the escort almost carry him down. His body seemed to be rigid as he was dragged to the chair and the Military Police had difficulty as they tied his limbs to the wooden legs and arms. Someone pinned a piece of white cloth over the man's chest and stepped back. In the anxiety to get the business over with the man had still not been blindfolded when the volley crashed out, its noise magnified by the quarry walls. "

Private P.J. Kennedy of the 18th Manchester Regiment was present at the execution of a British private for desertion.

FIRING SQUAD FACTS

- A total of 306 British and Empire soldiers were executed in World War I.
- The U.S. Army executed 35 soldiers in France, but for criminal rather than military offenses.
- The French executed more than 600 of their own soldiers; the Germans only executed 18 deserters.
- Military offenses punishable by death included desertion, cowardice, disobeying an order, and sleeping or being drunk on duty.
- Many men shot for cowardice or desertion are now believed to have been suffering from shell shock.

The Home Front

The U.S. government wanted to make the whole economy part of the war effort. It worked with labor unions to prevent strikes. It organized campaigns to get people to grow more food, and to use less meat, grain, gasoline, and coal. Many women took industrial jobs for the first time to replace men who were away fighting. The government raised funds through "Liberty Loans," which encouraged citizens to buy bonds to invest in the war effort.

Beat back the HUN with LIBERTY BONDS

The Liberty Bond campaign used posters like this image of a sinister German soldier, and also got Hollywood stars to promote bonds.

This U.S. poster uses the campaign against German U-boats to encourage support for the war.

THEY KEPT THE SEA LANES OPEN

INVEST IN THE VICTORY LIBERTY LOAN

66 This is the anniversary of our acceptance of Germany's challenge to fight for our right to live and be free, and for the sacred rights of free men everywhere. The nation is awake. There is no need to call to it. We know what the war must cost, our utmost sacrifice, the lives of our fittest men, and, if need be, all that we possess.

The loan we are met to discuss is one of the least parts of what we are called upon to give and to do, though in itself imperative. The people of the whole country are alive to the necessity of it, and are ready to lend [money] to the utmost, even where it involves a sharp skimping and daily sacrifice to lend out of meagre earnings. They will look with reprobation [disapproval] and contempt upon those who can and will not, upon those who demand a higher rate of interest, [and] upon those who think of it as a mere commercial transaction. 99

Woodrow Wilson made this speech to launch the third Liberty Loan campaign in April 1918 in Baltimore.

HOME FRONT FACTS

- There were five Liberty Loans in all.
- The loans raised about $17 billion— equivalent to about $170 per American.
- Poster and movie campaigns were used to encourage Americans to support the war effort; schools taught lessons in patriotism and nationalism.
- The Committe on Public Information was set up to control information. It trained "four-minute" men to make speeches encouraging support for the war.
- Many women went to work in industry to support the war effort; many more volunteered to help the Red Cross.

Keeping Up Morale

U.S. soldiers with members of the British Women's Army Auxiliary Corps (WAACs), who served in France.

It was vital to keep up morale among soldiers at the front. The Young Men's Christian Association (YMCA) set up recreation clubs for soldiers. Concert parties put on theatrical shows for their comrades. Not only did such shows help defeat boredom, they also made soldiers feel they had not been forgotten at home.

Injured Allied soldiers visit with women working in a munitions factory in France.

" My mother said I was going to see very cruel things and I must not worry, and [that] I had to be pleasant and smile. She said, 'You just have to say the poems that you usually say.' So she was introducing me saying, 'My daughter is going to read some poetry.' She said that my father was a soldier like them, so I was going to read them the poems that I thought were going to please my father.

So it was just poetry of the time, poems that were written for the soldiers only. It was just the idea that it was important that there were things written for them, especially seeing a young girl reading those poems. I was just like a child, and I was told that I had to be kind to them. So I kissed the ones that wanted me to give them a hug. "

Hermine Venot-Focké was a young Frenchwoman in Calais when she joined her mother visiting injured Allied soldiers.

MORALE FACTS

- The YMCA set up hundreds of clubs in the United States and Europe.
- The "Y" was a place where men could read, write letters, or go to dances.
- Volunteers also used trucks to deliver coffee and pastries to troops closer to the front lines.
- Many men missed female company. They socialized with WAACs, nurses, and other women working in France.
- Writing home and receiving mail was an important morale booster.
- Songs were also popular among soldiers; favorites included "Over There" and "It's a Long Way to Tipperary."

The End of the War

The U.S.-led Meuse–Argonne Offensive on the Westerm Front began on September 26, 1918, and made advances. On October 4, the Germans abandoned the defensive Hindenburg Line. By November 1, their resistance had collapsed. The Germans asked for peace. An armistice was arranged. It began at 11:00 A.M. on November 11, 1918.

French and U.S. military personnel in Paris celebrate the Armistice on November 11, 1918.

Hundreds of Doughboys arrive back in New York's port after the war.

> " The bells of London began to clash. The street was crowded with people in hundreds, nay, thousands, rushing hither and thither in a frantic manner, shouting and screaming with joy. Around me in our headquarters disorder had broken out. Doors banged. Feet clattered down corridors. Everyone rose from the desk and cast aside pen and paper. All bounds were broken.
>
> The tumult grew like a gale, but from all sides simultaneously. The street was now a seething mass of humanity. Flags appeared as if by magic. Streams of men and women flowed from the Embankment. They mingled with torrents pouring down from the Strand on their way to acclaim the King. Almost before the last stroke of the clock had died away, the strict, war-straitened, regulated streets of London had become a triumphant pandemonium. "

Winston Churchill was Britain's Minister for Munitions when the Armistice began on November 11, 1918.

VICTORY FACTS

- On October 5, the German government asked U.S. President Wilson to begin negotiations for them with the Allies.
- Negotiations broke down, but resumed on November 5.
- Revolution broke out in Germany; the Kaiser was forced to abdicate, and a new republic was announced.
- The guns on the Western Front fell silent at 11.00 A.M. on November 11: the 11th hour of the 11th day of the 11th month.
- The victors met in Paris in 1919 to decide the terms of the peace treaties.

GLOSSARY

abdicate When a ruler gives up a throne.

armistice An agreement between warring enemies to stop fighting, usually to agree to a surrender.

barrage A concentrated artillery bombardment over a large area.

battalion A large infantry unit ready for battle.

concert party A group of performers who stage variety shows.

conscription Compulsory enrollment in the armed services.

convoy A group of ships or vehicles all traveling together to the same destination, usually for protection.

dog fight A close combat between military aircraft.

fraternization Associating with the enemy in a friendly way.

mobilize To prepare and arm the military to be ready for active service.

morale The belief of a fighting force that it will eventually be victorious.

munitions Military weapons, ammunition, and other equipment.

peninsula A piece of land that is bordered by water on three sides.

propaganda Information created by governments to convince people that one cause is right or another is wrong.

prosthetics The design of artificial body parts.

reservist A member of a country's reserve armed forces who can be called on in times of emergency.

truce A temporary ceasefire between warring enemies.

U-boat Short for "Unterseeboot," which is German for submarine.

ultimatum A demand made by one country to another which will result in war if it is not met.

FURTHER INFORMATION

Books

Arthur, Max. *Forgotten Voices of the Great War*. Ebury Press, 2002.

Barber, Nicola. *World War I* (Living Through). Heinemann-Raintree, 2012.

Gregory, Josh. *World War I* (Cornerstones of Freedom). Scholastic, 2012.

Lewis, John E. *On the Front Line: True World War I Stories*. Constable, 2012.

Samuels, Charlie. *Machines and Weaponry of World War I* (Machines that Won the War). Gareth Stevens Publishing, 2013.

Samuels, Charlie. *Timeline of World War I* (Americans at War). Gareth Stevens, 2011.

Websites

www.worldwar1.com/
Commerical site with comprehensive coverage of the conflict, and a sub-site on the Trenches.

www.archives.gov/exhibits/eyewitness/
National Archives site of eyewitness accounts of key moments in U.S. history.

wwi.lib.byu.edu/
Archive of primary sources of World War I maintained by Brigham Young University.

www.pbs.org/greatwar/
Site to accompany the PBS series *The Great War*, with documentary footage and interviews.

Publisher's note to educators and parents: Our editors have carefully reviewed these websites to ensure that they are suitable for students. Many websites change frequently, however, and we cannot guarantee that a site's future contents will continue to meet our high standards of quality and educational value. Be advised that students should be closely supervised whenever they access the Internet.

INDEX